Willow Tree

Story/Illustrations
Jeanne Buesser

2015 ©Jeanne Buesser. All rights reserved.
No part of this book may be reproduced, stored in a retrieval system, or transmitted by any means without the written permission of the author.

Books by Jeanne Buesser

He Talks Funny

Moonlight Till Dawn

Journey From Darkness To Light Willow Tree

Water Line- *(not yet released)*

Gracefully it stands, swaying in the wind.
Small branches bend, though do not break.
Scarred trunk, gnarled roots, missing limbs...
Still it grows, gently moving as we stand in awe.

Years ago, in a grassy meadow lay the seed for a very small tree. On a distant hill some very large trees stood.

Mice, birds, chipmunks foraged for berries and seeds in the meadow grass; large birds soared high seeking prey below.

Smaller birds sought shelter from the hawk's eyes. The very small tree seed lay on a small patch of ground surrounded by grass, perhaps carried there by a wafting wind.

Sun shone on this brittle seed. Rain moistened the dry soil. As the seasons progressed changes occurred.

In spring, a gentle wind carried clouds across the sky. Butterflies fluttered from flower to flower.

Bees buzzed. Blades swayed. Rain added a sweet smell. Feeling fearful and afraid of hungry animals feasting on the grass, Willow hoped he wouldn't be stepped on.

Shallow roots, shoots and leaves emerged slowly.
Spring grass in the morning dew glimmered.
Days and nights rejoiced in the cool air.

Willow's roots gently dug into the soil and rock
trying to hold on, growing a little stronger everyday.

Other meadow flowers would show their
colors and the meadow grass changed from winter's
restful hue to brilliant green.

With branches reaching towards the sky, the tree continued growing. This very young tree looked across the meadow spying larger, older trees standing tall and majestic in the nearby hills.

There was no one like him. Willow sighed, feeling sad and lonely. He heard birds chirping, viewed animals roaming through the grass.

Might the fledgeling sustain the energy needed to grow? "Can I be like the large strong trees" he worried?

Willow began to cry as his small branches and delicate leaves quivered and shook.

Just then, he heard a voice in the wind. It was Mother Nature, who watches over all her earthly charges.

She whispered gently. "Don't cry little one. You will grow. It will take some time, my Willow". He stopped to listen. "Who said that?" he asked. No reply came.

The birds continued singing, and the winds blew by. After a time Willow ceased crying. Spring lasted a very long time!

Summer arrived. Warm sun beat down on the meadow. Grass sported brown. There was little rain.

Many animals stayed away as insufficient grass denied them food. In time, Willow grew stronger, sturdier, and taller.

Wispy leaves sprouted from wider branches, roots dug deeper into the soil. Towards summer's end Willow's leaves looked different turning from green to fall hues.

His trunk produced a layer of bark. It frightened him to consider what the next season would bring.

Weather can prove very powerful. The sky darkened with clouds as rainstorms with lightning strikes and fierce winds approached. Willow was so wet.

He heard tall trees twisting and cracking branches, observing what happened around him.

Many of the animals homes were blown away in the wind causing the meadow and trees to look quite different. Storm damage to the largest of trees, toppled them causing them to fall apart.

How scared Willow became as the meadow offered him no protection!

Years passed; the hills looked exceedingly different from when Willow first sprouted from a tiny seed.

When the storm subsided, a beautiful rainbow formed in the sky. The different colored leaves, in hues of reds, golds, browns, scattered on the ground.

They lay on the wet grass. The weather changed, becoming colder each day.

Winter brought blowing snow and raging winds.
The cold snow blanketed the meadow deeply.

Sometimes ice formed on the ground. The little animals found it hard to find their burrows or nests, so they might hide from the winter's wrath.

Willow swayed slowly, creaking and bending with the winds, while ice clung to the tree branches.

Finally, winter subsided, the snow and ice melted. Willow looked around at the remaining other trees.

Willow recalled days gone by and how he felt sadness and loneliness as a young tree. He remembered Mother Nature's talk promising growth, encouraging him to have patience.

After a while Willow smiled inside. He realized that the older, stronger, taller trees lacked his flexibility through storms, winds and the change of seasons. Willow survived!

Though different from others, Willow was the strongest tree of all!

Acknowledgments

To my Guardian Angels/those special friends who watch over me, I am grateful for their love and support. I look forward to meeting new friends on this journey.

A special thank you to Gwen, DC, Andrea who helped edit my stories.

Authors and friends who have made such a difference in my life, stuck by me. I want to thank Julie and Marc for editing and support through Edit911.com, as well as Dave at Alphagraphics.

To Dr. Mike, Betty and others as a member of their group on Facebook, Helping A Children's Author Out (HACAO), my thanks.

Jeanne Buesser

About the Author

Jeanne Buesser is an author, artist and poet she's President of the Apraxia Network for over 16 years. She resides in New Jersey with her two sons. Jeanne spent her childhood growing up with her family in Kenya, East Africa for 8 years.

Ms Buesser provides support/information via mail, email and phone for families of children diagnosed with a severe neurological speech disorder called Apraxia.

She has authored five books which also include resources. He Talks Funny, (Water Line pending), Willow Tree which are special needs. Poetry books on grief, Moonlight Till Dawn, Journey From Darkness To Light. They also provide resources for parents.

Books can be purchased online at Amazon.com, Barnesand Noble.com, BooksAmillion,com. Local libraries and schools also lend these books. Find Buesser on Linkedin, Facebook, Twitter, Youtube, Authorsden, AuthorCentral.
Jeanne Buesser's blogs are on Authorden and her website. Which are jeannebuesser.com, or apraxianetwork.org.

If you would like to defray the cost of shipping books to the CCDO in Tanzania, please send your donation to Jeanne Buesser c/o Apraxia Network, PO Box 1142, Paramus, NJ 07653-1142. Please write CCDO shipment donation in the memo area. A reciept will be mailed to you.

Further Information

An CCDO orphanage for children with reading disabilities or Aids. Shipping is expensive boxes/packages go by weight at least $15 to start. Locate books at local garage/library book sales, at booksales.org.

Children's Care Development Organization
(CCDO)

Majaliwa Mbogella- chairperson
Children Care Development Organization
PO Box 1751
Kihesa-iringa
Tanzania, East Africa

Non-profit Recommended Resources (special needs)

www.arcbergenpassaiccounties.org
www.easterseals.org
http://capabilityranch.org/
www.bcfriendship.com
www.j-add.org
 www.yachad.org
www.autismontheseas.com

No Kill Animal Shelter

http://rbari.org/
(special needs book store)
 http://wordsbookstore.com/category/events/ ...

Authors websites/resources

http://edit911.com
www.UnforgettableFacesandStories.com
http://cherryevasquez.tateauthor.com
Title: Books That Sow: Strength, Character & Diversity, DBA
www.funwithphonicstutoring.com
www.amitypublications.com
http://docprov.com
HACAO- (Helping A Children's Author Out)
http://www.BonnieFerrante.ca
http://www.acatofninetales.com
http://www.alphagraphics.com/
www.montecarlosolutions.com
www.asmsg.com

World organizations-Changing the World

http://www.heifer.org/beyond-hunger/index.html
http://www.awf.org/
http://www.israeltreex.org/
http://www.jnf.org/support/tree-planting-center/
http://www/hummingbirdsociety.org/index.php http://savebees.org/
http://www.saveourmonarchs.org/
http://thewaterproject.org/
http://www.savethewhales.org/

www.ingramcontent.com/pod-product-compliance
Lightning Source LLC
Chambersburg PA
CBHW041230040426
42444CB00002B/118